MW01241488

Green Living
No Action Too Small

by Lucia Raatma

Content Adviser: Teresa Kittridge, Executive Director,
Renewable Energy Marketplace—
Alliance for Talent Development

Science Adviser: Terrence E. Young Jr., M.Ed., M.L.S.,
Jefferson Parish (Louisiana) Public School System

Reading Adviser: Alexa L. Sandmann, Ed.D., Professor of Literacy,
College and Graduate School of Education, Health, and Human Services,
Kent State University

Compass Point Books
151 Good Counsel Drive
P.O. Box 669
Mankato, MN 56002-0669

This book was manufactured with paper containing
at least 10 percent post-consumer waste.

Photographs © All photos by Capstone Press/Karon Dubke except:
Corbis/Bob Sacha, 44–45; Royalty-Free/Tim Pannell, 51; Getty Images Inc./Chad Buchanan, 43; Vince Bucci,
57; iStockphoto/ericfoltz, 8–9; matteodestefano, 28; oldproof, 53; schnuddel, 30; Shutterstock/J. Breedlove,
33; Jan Martin Will, 12; Lisa F Young, 11; Liv friis-larsen, 49; maxstockphoto, 4, 6, 13, 26, 39, 48; Petr
Vaclavek, 29; Rafa Irusta, 7; RoJo Images, 34.

Editor: Jennifer VanVoorst
Designer: Heidi Thompson
Media Researcher: Wanda Winch
Art Director: LuAnn Ascheman-Adams
Creative Director: Joe Ewest
Editorial Director: Nick Healy
Managing Editor: Catherine Neitge

Library of Congress Cataloging-in-Publication Data
Raatma, Lucia.
  Green living : no action too small / by Lucia Raatma.
    p. cm. — (Green generation)
  Includes bibliographical references and index.
  ISBN 978-0-7565-4245-0 (library binding)
  ISBN 978-0-7565-4293-1 (paperback)
 1. Green movement—Juvenile literature. 2. Environmental
protection—Citizen participation—Juvenile literature.
I. Title. II. Series.
 GE195.5.R38 2010
 640—dc22   2009008779

Visit Compass Point Books on the Internet at *www.compasspointbooks.com*
or e-mail your request to *custserv@compasspointbooks.com*

Contents

Getting Warmer

introduction

Global warming. Climate change. You can seldom read the news these days without seeing these terms. What do they mean? Essentially Earth's temperature is rising. In fact the temperature has risen 1 degree Fahrenheit (0.6 degrees Celsius) in the last century. Some scientists predict that it may rise by 2 to 11.5 F (1.2 to 6.9 C) by 2100. This may not sound like a lot, but in reality it's huge. The planet has not changed this much in tens of thousands of years. Most scientists agree that this is a human-made problem caused by an increase in greenhouse gases in the atmosphere. These gases trap the sun's heat close to the planet's surface, causing Earth's temperature to rise. They are the result of pollution and carbon dioxide emissions that people create through everyday activities such as driving cars and making and using electricity.

Evidence of global warming includes melting glaciers and warmer weather. The future impact of global warming could include more severe weather, such as droughts, hurricanes, and heavy snowfall. Global warming could also lead to further spread of diseases, changes in animal populations, and destruction of coral reefs.

It may sound depressing—and overwhelming. You may wonder, "What can one person do to help?" The answer is: a lot. By making small changes every day in the way you live, you can save energy and conserve resources to help the planet remain healthy for generations to come. When your efforts are combined with those of other people, the results can be amazing. The world is our home, and there are many ways we can help take care of it.

Check It

Climate Fever

It's getting hot out there. Consider these alarming facts:

- More than one-fifth of the polar ice caps has melted since 1979.
- By 2030, scientists think, there may be no more glaciers in Montana's Glacier National Park.
- If the average temperature rises more than 4.5 F (2.4 C), nearly a quarter of all plant and animal species on Earth could be at risk of extinction.

> "My approach to green living is all about keeping it simple. Be mindful of the impact your actions leave behind, take responsibility for your actions, and have respect for the world around you."
> —Tyra Banks, model and talk show host

Why Go Green?

chapter 1

Human life on Earth has taken its toll, and it is up to us to reverse the course. We can make our world cleaner and greener. "Living green" may sound like a lot of work, but it's not. Everyday people can make the world better just by changing a few things in their lives.

Planet Earth relies on a number of natural resources to survive. Some of these are nonrenewable—there is a fixed amount that someday could run out. These nonrenewable resources include fossil fuels such as gasoline, coal, diesel fuel, and natural gas. Other resources are renewable, which means we can never run out. These include wind, sunlight, and tides.

So it is important to stop relying so much on nonrenewable resources. For one thing, burning fossil fuels is bad for the atmosphere. In addition, scientists predict that at our current rate of consumption, we will run out of fossil fuels in 40 to 70 years. Then what will we do? Many scientists are focusing their efforts on creating energy from renewable resources. They have harnessed the sun's energy for solar heating and lighting. They have built wind turbines, which supply energy for homes and businesses. They have begun working with hydropower, which relies on the movement of water in

Wind turbines capture energy from the wind and convert it to electricity.

lakes and rivers. All these are clean, renewable ways to provide energy.

The sun will always shine and the wind will always blow, but there is a fixed supply of water on Earth. Because the water cycle circulates water from the surface of Earth to the atmosphere and back, the water supply seems to

Hydroelectric dams create clean energy by converting the energy of moving water into electricity.

constantly renew itself. Still, pollution has made some freshwater undrinkable, and turning saltwater into drinking water is complicated and expensive. Droughts are symptoms of global warming. If the

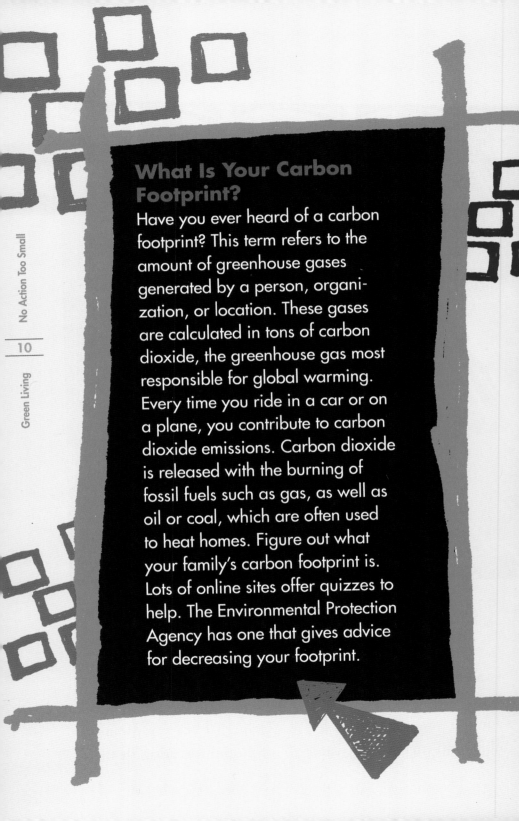

What Is Your Carbon Footprint?

Have you ever heard of a carbon footprint? This term refers to the amount of greenhouse gases generated by a person, organization, or location. These gases are calculated in tons of carbon dioxide, the greenhouse gas most responsible for global warming. Every time you ride in a car or on a plane, you contribute to carbon dioxide emissions. Carbon dioxide is released with the burning of fossil fuels such as gas, as well as oil or coal, which are often used to heat homes. Figure out what your family's carbon footprint is. Lots of online sites offer quizzes to help. The Environmental Protection Agency has one that gives advice for decreasing your footprint.

Human beings and many other living things need freshwater to survive.

climate continues to change, there may be less freshwater available for everyone to use. So even though the amount of water on Earth does not change, it is still important to conserve this resource.

Trees are another important resource. The planet has lots of trees, and we can always plant more. However, when forests are destroyed for new farms, homes, and businesses, natural areas are lost. Trees provide shade, and they are homes to many animals. They also take in carbon dioxide and emit oxygen, so they make the air cleaner. Life on Earth requires healthy forests. We have to make an effort to keep green places green.

There is a saying from Kenya: "Treat the earth well. It was not given to you by your parents. It was loaned to you by your children." It may be difficult to look ahead like that, but give it a try. Imagine what the world will be like for your kids and grandkids if you don't help save it today. There may be a shortage of freshwater, or entire species of animals could become extinct. If the glaciers melt, the seas will rise, and land we have today may end up under water.

Life on Earth relies on a delicate balance of resources. When things are out of balance, life is threatened. The good news is that you can help! Through small changes in the way you live every day, you can do your part to help preserve the planet and bring it back into balance.

> "I take a three-minute shower. ... I even brush my teeth when I shower. Now here's why. I found out that every two minutes in the shower uses as much water as a person in Africa uses for everything in their life for a whole day—drinking, bathing, cooking, and cleaning ... everything!"
> —Jennifer Aniston, actress

It All Starts at Home

chapter 2

Take a minute to look around your home, and consider this: There are about 100 million homes in the United States, and each person creates about 4.5 pounds (2 kilograms) of garbage each day. That's about 135 pounds (61 kg) per person each month! Right now if you combined all the landfills in the United States, they would take up space equal to the state of Pennsylvania.

In addition, you and your family probably use many gallons of water each day and lots of electricity. Talk to your family members about how you can cut down on waste and make your home more energy efficient. Saving the planet starts at home. Here are some ways to help.

Recycle: This is a big one! Look for the recycling symbol on items you're done with, and be sure to recycle them. These are usually glass and plastic bottles, aluminum cans, and plastic packaging. You can also recycle newspapers, magazines, and paper. Some communities offer curbside pickups of items for recycling, but other places require you to drop them off. Find out what your town's rules are, and make the effort to deposit

The U.S. Environmental Protection Agency estimates that Americans recycle about a third of their waste.

recyclables in the right place. If everyone in the United States recycled, landfills would be 75 percent smaller. Get your whole family on board!

Turn off the water: Don't let

the water run while you brush your teeth or shave. There's no need for gallons of unused water to go down the drain. Also take shorter showers. A 10-minute shower may feel great, but you can get clean faster than that! Challenge family members to see who can take the fastest shower.

Fix leaks: With your

family's help, check for leaks in your home. If a faucet or toilet has a leak, you could be wasting a gallon or more

Check It

Recycle It!

Take a look at this list of commonly recycled items and contact your local recycling center with any questions.

- glass containers (both clear and colored)
- office paper
- newsprint (used for newspapers)
- glossy paper (used for magazines)
- cardboard
- aluminum and steel cans
- plastics

of water a day. Get the leak repaired. If there are spaces around windows and doors, get them sealed to prevent hot or cool air from escaping and driving up energy use in the home.

Hand wash: Whenever

possible, hand wash delicate items instead of taking them to the dry cleaner. Most dry cleaners use harsh chemicals that remain on your clothes, which you then inhale. Or try to find a dry cleaner that uses more environmentally friendly materials.

Run full loads: Make sure your dishwasher is full before you run it. There's no need to use all that water for just a few glasses or dishes. The same goes for your washing machine: Wait for a full load of clothes before you turn it on. Also use cold water. Most of the time, it cleans just as well as hot water, and using it saves energy.

Let it dry: When you can, hang your laundry outside to dry. You'll save energy, and your clothing will smell great. Also set your dishwasher to air dry. There's no need to waste energy on dishes that will dry by themselves.

Save water and energy by washing only full loads and then hanging the wet clothes outside to dry.

Use the tap: Bottled water may be convenient, but all that plastic really adds up. Drink tap water instead. If you are worried about your water quality, talk to your family about installing a water filter. It's cheaper than buying all that drinking water from the supermarket, and nothing ends up in the landfill.

Cook smart: When you cook on the stove, be sure to use the right size burner for the job. A small pot on a large burner wastes energy. Also, if you have one, use a toaster oven to cook small meals. It uses less energy than a big oven.

Watch your plate: Don't serve yourself more food than you will eat. That just creates waste. When dining out, don't order more than you need. If you have leftovers, take them home for the next day's lunch.

Try composting: This may sound a little too "down to earth," but give it a try! Instead of throwing them in the trash, put fruit and vegetable scraps, eggshells, and coffee grounds in a compost bin. Then use the compost for fertilizing your yard or garden. It cuts down on trash, and the compost makes your yard greener.

Forget plastic foam: Styrofoam is forever—nearly. Nobody knows how long it takes for plastic foam to break down in a landfill, but it's certainly many hundreds of years.

Eco-friendly Homes

If you and your family are building a new house or renovating an old one, there may be ways to go green. Talk to your parents about making your home more energy efficient. Perhaps you can add more insulation to keep your home warmer in the winter and cooler in the summer. If you're replacing appliances, consider upgrading to those marked Energy Star, which are now widely available. If windows need to be replaced, install double-paned ones, which keep drafts under control. Consider low-flow toilets, which use less water. If your family is really committed, you could install solar panels so your home gets energy from the sun.

That's hundreds of years of toxic substances' being leached into the ground-water! If you really need a disposable cup, use a paper one, which is biodegradable. Better yet, use a ceramic or glass mug.

Use less paper: Got a
spill? Reach for a sponge or a cloth towel, not a paper one. Opt for real plates and cups, not those you throw away. Use less toilet paper and fewer napkins. Print on both sides of office paper, and use old paper for scribbling notes. Think of the trees: The less paper people use, the fewer trees will be cut down to produce it. You'll be amazed at how much you can save.

Go paperless: You can
also encourage your parents to go paperless. They can get their paychecks deposited directly into their bank accounts. They can pay bills online, and they can opt not to request receipts from ATM withdrawals. All these paper-free habits add up.

Forget phone books:
With your parents' permission, call your local phone company and ask to be taken off the list for phone book delivery. Phone books can be huge and hard to handle, and they make up 10 percent of the waste in landfills. You can get phone numbers from the Internet.

Check your thermostat: During the
cold months, lower your heat a degree or two, and wear a sweater if you're cold. Just a small change will save electricity and lower your family's monthly bill. In the summer, raise your

thermostat a degree or two to save energy on air-conditioning. If you're warm, dress light, and try a floor or ceiling fan to keep the air moving.

Think before you flush: The average toilet uses 4.5 gallons (17 liters) of water for each flush. Cut down on flushing when you can, and reduce the amount of water used per flush by placing a water-filled plastic jug in the toilet tank. This will take up space so that less water will be needed to refill the tank after a flush. Never flush unnecessarily. Using several gallons of water to get rid of an item that could simply be put in the trash is quite wasteful.

Flushing the toilet accounts for about 19 percent of water use in American homes.

Turn it off: You can save energy with just the flick of a switch! When you leave a room, turn out the lights. When you're done with the TV, turn that off, too. There's no need to have a bright room with no one it in. There's no need to have the TV blaring if no one is watching, either. If you want a light on when you come home at night, talk to your family about installing a timer so a light's not burning for hours unnecessarily.

Recharge your batteries:
Think of all the batteries you use over the course of a year. Instead of constantly buying new ones, try rechargeable ones. You can use these over and over, which keeps more batteries from being discarded.

Unplug it: Did you know that many appliances and other electronics use electricity even when they are turned off? The solution is to unplug items you aren't using. That may be tough if the TV is plugged into an outlet behind a huge entertainment center. However, you can plug items into a power strip and then turn off the power strip when you aren't using them. The power strip doesn't draw power when it's off.

Open the windows:
On nice days when you don't need your furnace or air conditioner, open the windows and let the fresh air in. It will clear your head and clear your home of stale air. It's much better than a fan, and there's no energy source required!

In most homes, the refrigerator consumes more energy than any other kitchen appliance.

Close the door: Be sure to close the refrigerator door after you've retrieved what you need. Leaving it standing open is a huge energy waster. If the heat or air-conditioning is on, be sure to close the door to your home, too. You don't want to lose all that warm or cold air and hike up your energy bill.

Change your lightbulbs: Next time a lightbulb burns out and needs changing, try a different kind. Compact fluorescent lightbulbs that meet Energy Star requirements use 75 percent less energy than standard lightbulbs, and they can last more than 10 times as long. They may cost a little more to buy, but they will quickly save a family about 12 percent off its electricity bill. If every home in the United States replaced just one standard bulb with a CFL, that would save enough energy to light more than 3 million homes for a year. It would also prevent greenhouse gas emissions equal to that of 800,000 cars. One note of caution: If a CFL breaks, be careful when disposing of it. Check the manufacturer's instructions.

By the Numbers

Hours and Hours

Look how a standard incandescent bulb compares with a CFL:

Bulb	Typical life span
CFL	6,000–15,000 hours
standard	750–1,000 hours

Check your medications:

If your medicine has expired, don't dump it down the drain. This puts antibiotics, pain relievers, and all sorts of other things into the water supply. Don't throw them in the garbage, either. You don't want drugs to get into the soil. Instead ask your local pharmacy or recycling center about recycling programs for medicine.

Check It

Recycle With Care

These items are just a few of the many household items considered hazardous. Check with your local recycling center for the best ways to dispose of them. Don't ever just throw them away!

- used motor oil
- leftover paint
- expired medications
- dead batteries
- electronic equipment

Reduce junk mail:

Get together with your family and see what mail you get each week. No doubt you receive a lot of junk mail — letters, catalogs, and flyers, all trying to sell you something. What can you do to stop it? One way is to register with the National Do Not Mail list. This service may not get your family off every list,

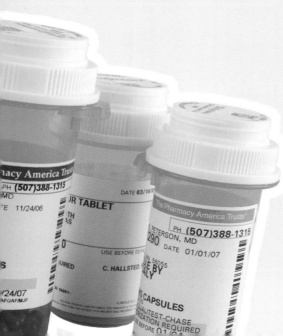

but it's a start. You can also call the toll-free numbers of the companies that send you junk mail and ask to be removed from their lists. Think of all the paper that can be saved!

If you set your mind to it, you can find lots of ways to make your home a greener place. Enlist the help of your family, and make a plan to save energy and keep your home healthy. Don't worry if you can't do everything at once. Try something new each week or even each day, and see what you can accomplish.

It's hard to stop the stream of junk mail completely, so make sure to recycle what you do receive.

"*I absolutely love our Prius. In addition to being obviously economical and environmentally friendly, they drive great. ... There's no reason all Americans shouldn't be driving hybrid cars.*"
—Will Ferrell, actor

The Secrets of Shopping

chapter 3

Shopping can be a lot of fun. You can find bargains and hang out with your friends in the process. But are you paying attention to what you buy? Many products are filled with chemicals that are bad for you and the environment. Some products are just energy-wasters. See what you can do to ramp up the quality of your purchases. Here are some ideas.

Go hybrid: You may not own a car yet, but you might be able to steer your family toward a more energy-efficient car. Next time your family is in the market for a new car, encourage your parents to consider a hybrid. Hybrid cars combine a gasoline engine and an electric motor. They use a lot less gas and are better for the planet. Keep an eye out for more innovative cars being invented as well. Cars that run solely on electricity or hydrogen may be in our future.

By the Numbers

How Far Does It Go?

Take a look at these miles-per-gallon estimates for vehicles currently on the market. The Camry is a best-selling mid-size sedan from Toyota, and the Escape is a sport utility vehicle from Ford. The hybrid versions of these vehicles may cost a little more up front, but think of the gasoline they will save!

Automobile	List price	Mpg: city	Mpg: hwy
Toyota Camry	$19,145	21	31
Toyota Camry Hybrid	$26,150	33	34
Ford Escape	$20,435	20	28
Ford Escape Hybrid	$29,645	34	31

Try organic: Most fruits and vegetables are sprayed with chemicals that kill insects. It turns out those chemicals are not just bad for insects. They can also be bad for the environment—and for you. They can get into the crops you eat and the water you drink, and they can stay in the soil for many years. Organic food is grown without the use of such chemicals, and many people say organic food just tastes better. Talk to your family about buying organic foods at the local supermarket, health food store, or farmers market.

Shopping at a farmers market has the added benefit of allowing you to meet the people who grow your food.

What Does Organic Really Mean?

For many years, lots of products were labeled organic. These days, however, there are tougher standards for getting an organic label. Basically, organic means that a product was grown without pesticides and artificial fertilizers and that a manufactured product has no additives. Most organic foods are grown at organic farms. Because they do not use pesticides, these farms do not release dangerous chemicals into the air. Most organic farms also use less energy than conventional farms.

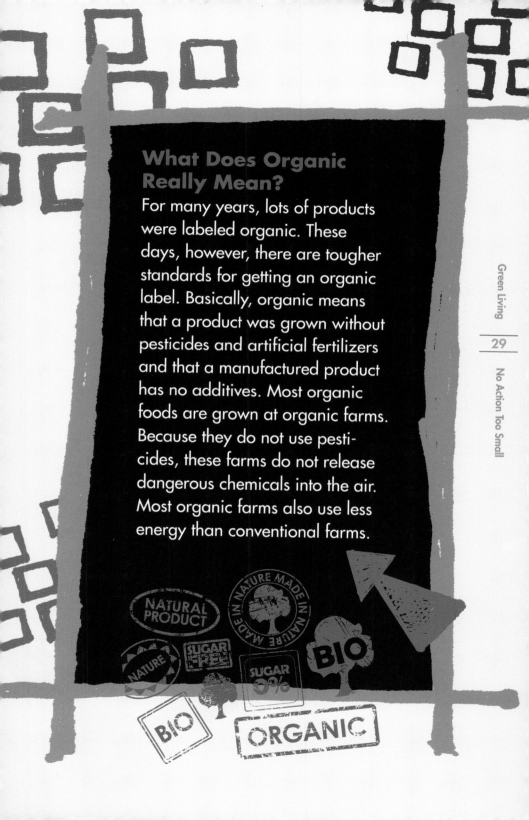

Buy in season: When you're buying fruits and vegetables, focus on what's in season. You may be able to get in-season produce from local farmers, which means that less energy is used to transport it.

Opt for less packaging: Some store items are packaged in huge boxes or plastic casing. Try to avoid those products and opt for less packaging. Packaging takes energy to produce and just leads to excess trash.

Buy in bulk: When you can, buy a large container of an item rather than lots of small ones. Less energy is used to produce one large container, and there will be less for you to recycle or throw out later.

Avoid processed food: If it comes in a box or a bag, take a moment to consider your purchase. Fresh foods are more healthful and don't contain preservatives and other chemicals, and since they usually need little or no packaging, they create less waste.

Reconsider meat: Lots of people love a good burger or steak, but consider this: The international meat industry produces about 18 percent of the world's greenhouse gas emissions. How? Cattle emit a gas called methane through their digestive process. This gas is natural for the cattle, but it is bad for the air. The more humans eat meat, however, the more demand there is for farmers to raise cattle. If you aren't ready to be a

vegetarian, be a flexitarian — make a conscious effort to cut back on the amount of meat you eat.

Try soy: There are lots of great foods these days that are made from soybeans. Soy products such as tofu are high in protein and are often eaten in place of meat. They are lower in calories and fat than meat, and growing soybeans uses less water than raising livestock.

Soy milk is healthful and comes in flavors such as chocolate and vanilla.

Check the label: If you can't pronounce most of the ingredients on a label, it probably isn't good for you. This is true for food as well as for cleaners and cosmetics. Many of those chemicals are bad for the environment, and you shouldn't be eating them, inhaling them, or rubbing them on your skin. Give nontoxic products a try. Some of these use basic natural ingredients that really do a good job. Better yet …

Go natural: Next time you're shopping, pick up some white vinegar. It kills mold and cuts through grease. Try baking soda for soap scum and other yucky situations. Natural products work just as well for basic cleaning, and they won't hurt the environment.

Skip aerosols: Air fresheners, cleaners, and hair sprays are sometimes packaged in aerosol cans. Yet aerosols sometimes contain materials that are bad for the atmosphere, and few recycling programs accept the canisters. Skip aerosols if possible.

Rethink bags: Paper or plastic? Neither one! When a clerk offers you a bag, try to do without if you can, especially if you have just one item. If you're grocery shopping with your family, bring reusable bags from home. Plastic bags are produced from oil, a nonrenewable fossil fuel, and they sit in landfills for years. Paper bags come from trees, which the planet needs. Try not to use disposable bags.

Ditch disposables:

Disposable items may be handy, but they just add to landfills. Try reusable lunch bags instead of paper ones.

Cloth napkins can make lunch feel like a special event, and they can be washed and reused again and again.

Download: Maybe you're

dying for that new CD. But are you just going to copy it onto your MP3 player? If so, it's cheaper to download the tunes from an online music

Because they are not exposed to air or moisture, items in a landfill decompose more slowly than in other conditions.

store. That means one less CD will end up in a landfill years from now.

Give less: That doesn't mean you shouldn't be generous. Instead give items such as gift cards or concert tickets, which cuts down on packaging. Make something yourself, such as baked goods or crafts. Or give an hour of your time to someone who needs it. Giving your time—or something you took the time to create—has more meaning than something you buy at a store. It's better for the environment, too.

Buy recycled: Help save trees by looking for paper products made from recycled paper. These include toilet paper and paper towels, as well as paper for your

Cookies are a great homemade gift. Most everyone likes them, and they're fun to make.

printer. Recycled paper is used in books (including this one!), magazines, and stationery. There are also great products made from recycled rubber and glass. Read those labels!

Buy used: Need a great dress or a cool sports coat for a special occasion? Looking for an interesting pair of shoes or a unique purse? Ditch the department store and head to a thrift store instead. You never know what you might find. Buying used clothing cuts down on consumption and can be cheaper, too!

Buying used clothing and donating old items when you're finished with them are other great ways to recycle.

Buy less: Before you make a purchase, take a moment to ask yourself whether you really need it. Do you really need three shades of nail polish, or is one enough? If your best friend has a video game you want to play, do you need a copy, too?

There may be some books and movies that you want to own, but if it's something you plan to read or watch just once, hit the library. Borrowing books and movies is free, and there will be no waste when you are done.

Get to know your local library. It's a great free resource for books, magazines, movies, and music.

Buy what you'll use:

You probably don't need two pairs of new shoes, even if there is a buy-one-get-one-free sale. No matter the size of your family, the jumbo size of mayonnaise will likely go bad before you can finish it. So shop with a friend and split your purchases.

Go online: With your
parents' permission, try shopping online. You'll save

money and time. If you want to send greeting cards, try e-cards instead of paper ones. They can be fun — and they'll never end up in a landfill.

When shopping, take your time. Don't get caught up in fads. Ignore all those impulse buys at the checkout counters. Really consider what you're spending money on. If you and others stop buying products that are bad for the planet, companies may stop making them. Try to buy items that are the best for you and for the environment.

Check It

Do I Need It?

It's easy to get caught up in shopping. Stores have sales, and online sites are fun. But you can be a smarter shopper. Next time, before you buy, ask yourself these questions:

- Do I really need it, or do I just want it?
- Will I still like it in six months?
- If I had to save for a month before I bought it, would I still want it?
- How many hours would I have to work (baby-sitting, doing yard work, etc.) to be able to pay for this? Is it worth it?

> "My grandmother ... raised her own vegetables in her backyard. I watched [her] reuse tinfoil. ... And when she was finished with a loaf of bread, she kept the plastic bag and she would use it for something. Nothing went to waste."
> —Cameron Diaz, actress

Reusing and Recycling

chapter 4

Recycling your bottles, cans, and newspapers is great for the environment. But there are other ways to recycle and reuse. The more you do, the less that ends up in landfills. Challenge yourself to come up with new uses for things you might otherwise throw away. Try these.

Boxes: Of course you can recycle the cardboard. But if you're feeling creative, try turning old boxes into treasure chests or storage bins. Decorate the boxes with pages from old magazines, calendars, and catalogs. Then use them for organizing all kinds of items—baseball cards, hair accessories, CDs, DVDs—you name it!

Plastic containers:

Keep them for rubber bands, paper clips, marbles, and other small items. They help keep things neat and tidy.

Plastic bags:

If you have a collection from the grocery store, don't add to it! Use the bags for other things. Take them to the beach or pool for wet clothing. Use them for dirty laundry when you're traveling. Scrunch them up to serve as packing material when mailing a package. Or use them over and over again at your supermarket.

Old clothing:

When you've outgrown clothing, find a place to donate your items. Maybe younger siblings, neighbors, or cousins can use them. If not, bag the clothing up and offer it to a charity that collects clothing for people in need. Even if a piece of clothing is really ratty, don't throw it out. Just use it to polish furniture or wash the car.

Books:

Is your home full of books that you read when you were younger? When you're finished with books, find a new home for them. Check with younger neighbors or relatives and see whether they would like your old reads. Or donate them to a local library.

How Long Does It Last?

When you throw an item in the trash, it doesn't really go away. You're just relocating it—to a landfill. Items can stay in landfills for a few weeks or a few thousand years before decomposing. Here's how long it takes for some common items—many of which can be recycled instead—to break down:

Item	Decomposition time
banana	3–4 weeks
paper bag	1 month
cotton rag	5 months
wool sock	1 year
leather shoe	40–50 years
rubber sole of shoe	50–80 years
aluminum can	200–500 years
plastic jug	1 million years
Styrofoam cup	unknown; possibly forever
glass bottle	unknown; possibly forever

Wrapping paper: It can be pretty, but wrapping paper is such a waste. It's used only once, and most wrapping paper can't be recycled. If you need to wrap a gift, try to reuse paper from gifts you've been given, or try making your own. Use paper from old catalogs or magazines. Or if you'd rather not wrap at all, try using reusable gift bags.

Athletic equipment: If you're finished with tennis, take your old racquet to a local court for someone else to use. No longer need your old baseball glove? Check with the local Little League. If your cleats are too small, give them to a younger player. Someone can always use the items you no longer need.

Gift wrap made from the comics section of the paper is both funny and recyclable.

Get to Know Ed Begley Jr.

You've probably seen Ed Begley Jr. on TV or in movies. One of his best-known roles was in *St. Elsewhere*, a show that was on in the 1980s. Since then, he's been on *Boston Legal*, *Scrubs*, and other programs. He also hosts *Living with Ed*, a reality show about his efforts to live a more environmentally friendly lifestyle. Begley first became interested in protecting the environment in the 1970s. Now he has his own garden, he composts and recycles, and he even bikes to fancy Hollywood parties. His home is equipped with solar panels and a small wind turbine. He even has created an all-purpose nontoxic cleaning product called Begley's Best.

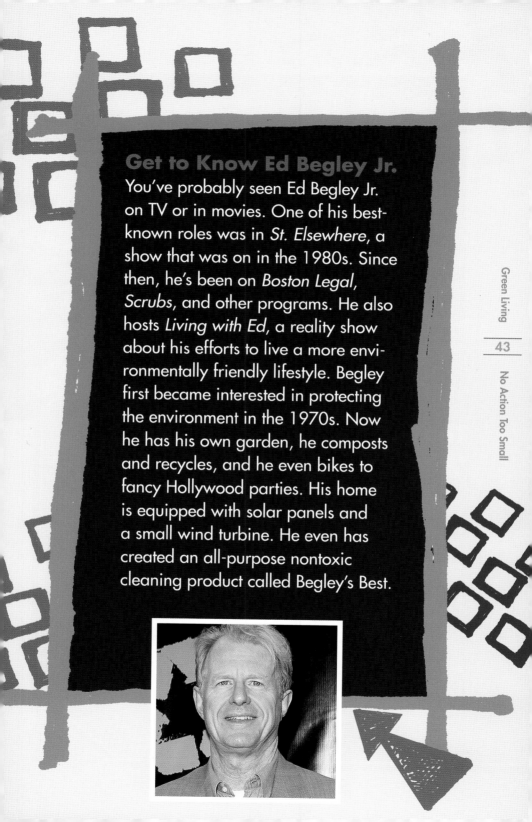

By the Numbers

The Value of Recycling

- 500,000 trees—These could be saved if every U.S. household replaced just one regular roll of paper towels with a recycled roll.
- 9 cubic yards (6.8 cubic meters)—This is the amount of landfill space saved by recycling 1 ton (0.9 metric tons) of cardboard.
- 5 percent—This is the amount of energy used to recycle an aluminum can versus making a new one.
- $160 million—This is the value of the world's recycling industry, which provides jobs for 1.5 million people.

According to recent government estimates, just 18 percent of discarded computers are collected for recycling.

Computers: If you think you need a new computer, consider a few things. Can your old one be fixed or upgraded? If so, that's cheaper than buying a new one, and it's certainly more environmentally friendly. But if you really need a new computer, figure out what to do with your old one. Some companies will take it off your hands to use for parts. Some organizations may welcome an old computer to refurbish. Or ask at your local recycling center about how to recycle it. Never put an old computer — or any electronic equipment — in the garbage. Many electronics components contain materials such as lead and mercury, which endanger people's health and the environment if dumped in landfills.

Cell phones: When you and your family get new cell phones and no longer need your old ones, donate them. Lots of organizations recycle the phones or reprogram them for people to use in emergencies.

Eyeglasses: Have a new prescription? Don't toss out your old glasses. Find out about programs that give old eyeglasses to people in need. One is called Give the Gift of Sight, which is sponsored by Lions Clubs and LensCrafters.

Ink cartridges: When your printer needs more ink, what do you do? There are two green options. You can recycle the cartridge, or you can refill it. Many manufac-turers supply postage-paid envelopes so you can return the cartridges for reuse or recycling. Some schools offer recycling programs, so check them out. Also, many companies now refill cartridges, which saves you money. Whatever you do, don't just throw the empty cartridges in the trash.

Use your imagination when it comes to recycling and reusing. Never throw anything out before giving it a good look and asking, "What else can I use this for?" And here's another challenge: Try to go a whole day—or a whole week—without buying anything new (except food). See how it feels to make do with what you already have on hand. You'll be surprised by what you come up with.

Tired-out Tires

What do people do with old tires when they get new ones for their cars? Let's hope they don't just send them to a landfill. Some people have gotten really creative and turned old tires into planters and even chairs. Some companies make sandals and handbags from recycled tires, and others make rubber mats and playground equipment. How would you recycle a tire?

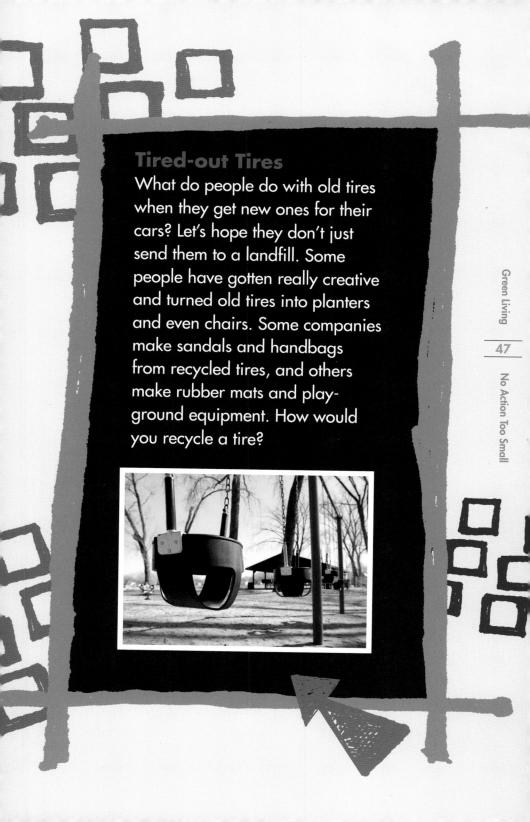

> "I think the environment should be put in the category of our national security. Defense of our resources is just as important as defense abroad. Otherwise what is there to defend?"
> —Robert Redford, actor and producer

Taking It Outside

chapter 5

The next time you're outside, stop for a moment. Close your eyes, and take a deep breath. Feel the breeze, and pay attention to how the air smells. Do you hear birds or just lots of traffic? Then open your eyes and look around. The world around us is amazing. Whether you're in a huge forest or a little city park, the green spaces in our lives are worth protecting and preserving. Here are some ways you can help.

Plant a garden: If you have a backyard, ask your parents about making part of it into a garden.

Green Living

49

No Action Too Small

Many people find it very satisfying to eat food they grew themselves.

You can plant tomatoes, cucumbers, squash, and herbs—whatever suits you! There are few things more satisfying than biting into a food you have grown with your own two hands. Be sure to use the compost from your kitchen to make your garden healthy. If you don't have a yard, you can still grow vegetables and other plants in pots on a balcony or patio, or in another sunny spot. Use your imagination! By planting your own garden, you're cutting down on purchases and making your home a little more green.

Install a rain barrel:

Talk to your parents about buying a rain barrel for your home. The barrel collects water when it rains that you can use later to water your yard and garden.

Set your sprinklers: If

your family uses a sprinkler system, talk to your parents about its settings. Be sure the sprinklers are on only in early mornings to help avoid excess evaporation, and install a rain shut-off to eliminate unnecessary watering. Water your lawn for long periods a couple of times each week, rather than every day, to allow deep penetration of the water. Avoid watering paved areas, and be sure to follow any local guidelines for days to water.

Avoid pesticides: Find

out what products are being used on your lawn. If your

Check It

Recycling for Growth

When you're ready to start a garden, these items are great for planting seedlings:
- egg cartons
- strawberry and grape tomato baskets
- old boots and shoes
- plastic bottles
- ice cream containers
- takeout food containers

family is using chemical pesticides, suggest that they try something greener. Check out natural alternatives at home improvement stores. There are lots of options these days.

Make your cookouts

green: Lots of families enjoy cooking out in the warm months. But burning charcoal briquettes releases substances that pollute the air—and may cause cancer. Instead use propane gas for your grill or use an electric grill. Offer lots of grilled vegetables and try to avoid paper plates. Try plastic plates or utensils that can be washed and reused.

Clean up a park: Is there a park in your community that could use some help? Talk to your teachers or parents about organizing a cleanup. You can throw away garbage and pull weeds. You can ask local authorities to have equipment repaired. All these efforts will make your neighborhood cleaner and the environment healthier.

Get your friends together to help clean up a public space. Doing good is even more fun with good company!

Greening Your School

You spend a lot of time at your school each day. How green is it? Find out what kind of lightbulbs your school has installed. Check out what kinds of cleaners the janitors use. Talk to your teachers or principal about ways to make your school more green. Perhaps the thermostat could be adjusted to save energy. Recycling bins could be added to classrooms and the cafeteria, if there aren't any already. There are lots of ways to save energy in your school. It's good for the environment, and your principal will like finding ways to save money!

A single tree creates 260 pounds (117 kg) of oxygen a year. That's a year's supply for two people.

Plant a tree: The last Friday in April is Arbor Day, a national observance that encourages tree planting and care. But don't wait for Arbor Day to plant a tree — or two or three. Trees are great for the environment because they take in carbon dioxide, which makes our air cleaner, and produce oxygen, which we breathe. They also provide shade on warm days. So add a few trees to your yard. Or check with community leaders about planting trees along streets and in parks.

Ride a bike or walk:

Think about the number of times you get in a car every day. Is there a way to do that less often? If you live close enough to school, maybe you could walk or ride a bike. Or if you're just going to a nearby friend's house, don't have someone drive you. Hop on your bike or slip on your sneakers and walk. Every time you opt not to take the car, you're saving gasoline and cutting down on harmful emissions.

Riding a bike is not just good exercise—it helps cut down on consumption of fossil fuels, and it's fun, too.

Go together: If you can't bike or walk where you need to go, try mass transit. By using public buses or trains, you're keeping more cars off the road and cutting down on traffic. No buses or trains in your area? Then give carpooling a try. See if you can combine car trips with others in your neighborhood.

If you're waiting in the car, turn the engine off. You can still listen to the radio even if the engine's not running.

Turn off the engine:

If you're traveling by car, encourage the driver to turn it off when possible. If you're waiting in a parking lot, don't idle the engine. An idling car just wastes gas and adds to the pollution in the air. If you're stuck in really bad traffic, it also makes sense to turn the engine off for a bit. Check your state's laws about this, though. In some states it's illegal to shut off the engine while on the road.

Don't litter: This may sound obvious, but never throw garbage on the ground or out a car window. Sometimes people can be

Get to Know Leonardo DiCaprio

He's starred in dozens of movies and appeared on countless magazine covers, but Leonardo DiCaprio is more than just a pretty face. He drives a hybrid car and lives in a solar-powered house. In 1998 he created the Leonardo DiCaprio Foundation, which enables him to use his star power to draw attention to environmental concerns. He has also produced and narrated a documentary called *The 11th Hour: Turn Mankind's Darkest Hour Into Its Finest*, which examines the looming environmental crisis and what people can do to help the planet.

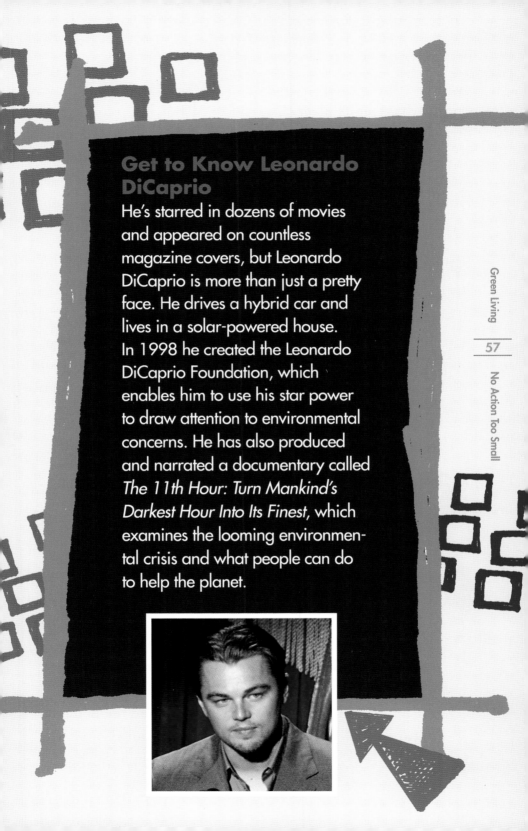

careless, but it's important to put garbage in its place. Use trash cans, and recycle what you can. Your world will be cleaner and more attractive, and the environment will be healthier.

Play during the day:

If you can, play baseball, tennis, and other sports during daylight hours. Lighting outdoor courts and fields uses up lots of energy, and it can be very costly.

Bring your own water:

When you're out for the day, bring your own water in a reusable water bottle. This cuts down on the disposable plastic water bottles that you buy from a vending machine or store. It's cheaper, too.

Enjoy the great outdoors:

Go to the park, have a picnic, or take a long hike. Just get out and appreciate the natural world around you. The more you see of your planet, the more you will want to protect it. Just be sure to leave these areas as you found them. Don't pick flowers or leave garbage behind. It is important to keep parks and forests clean for others to use as well.

Book an eco-trip:

Next time your family is ready for a vacation, consider an environmentally friendly one. Eco-tourism promotes environmental awareness and may introduce you to places that are less crowded—and really interesting. You can also try eco-friendly hotels. They

Having a picnic with your friends is a great way to enjoy the outdoors.

usually have the same prices as other hotels, but they use less water and energy.

Get involved: Want to do more? Find an environmental organization that needs your help. One is the Student Conservation Asso-ciation. This group uses high school and college volunteers to preserve parks, forests, refuges, and other green spaces throughout the United States. Other important organizations include the Natural Resources Defense Council and Global Green USA.

Between school and your
responsibilities at home,
you probably have a really
busy life. Just don't forget
to take time to be good to
your planet. Little things
every day can make your
world a greener and better

Working with others to protect the environment increases both your impact and your enjoyment.

place. Challenge yourself to find ways to help. Set a good example for those around you, and — who knows? — maybe you will inspire others to go green, too.

Glossary

atmosphere — blanket of gases that surrounds a planet

biodegradable — able to decay and be absorbed by the environment

carbon dioxide — greenhouse gas most responsible for global warming

carbon footprint — measure of the amount of carbon dioxide produced by a person, organization, or location at a given time

compost — mixture of decayed organic matter that is used for fertilizing

eco-friendly — not harmful to the environment

emissions — substances released into the air

fossil fuels — fuels, including coal, oil, and natural gas, made from the remains of ancient organisms

global warming — rise in the average worldwide temperature of Earth's atmosphere

greenhouse gases — gases in a planet's atmosphere that trap energy from the sun

hybrid — vehicle that runs on more than one source of power; most hybrid vehicles run on gasoline and electricity

landfill — place where garbage is disposed of by being buried beneath layers of dirt

natural resources — substances found in nature that people use, such as soil, air, trees, coal, and oil; some are renewable, while others have a fixed supply

organic — grown without the use of chemical fertilizers, pesticides, or other artificial substances

pesticides — substances, usually chemical, applied to crops to kill harmful insects and other creatures

Investigate Further

MORE BOOKS TO READ

Amsel, Sheri. *The Everything Kids' Environment Book.* Avon, Mass.: Adams Media, 2007.

Coley, Mary McIntyre. *Environmentalism: How You Can Make a Difference.* Mankato, Minn.: Capstone Press, 2009.

Hall, Julie. *A Hot Planet Needs Cool Kids.* Bainbridge Island, Wash.: Green Goat Books, 2007.

Thornhill, Jan. *This Is My Planet: The Kids' Guide to Global Warming.* Toronto: Maple Tree Press, 2007.

INTERNET SITES

FactHound offers a safe, fun way to find Internet sites related to this book. All of the sites on FactHound have been researched by our staff.

Here's all you do:
Visit *www.facthound.com*
FactHound will fetch the best sites for you!

Index

About the Author

Lucia Raatma has written dozens of books for young readers. They are about famous people, historical events, ways to stay safe, and many other topics. She lives in Florida's Tampa Bay area with her husband and their two children. They take their recycling items to the curb every other Wednesday.